WILD
WEATHER TRIVIA

By Kristin Palmer

Gareth Stevens
Publishing

Please visit our website, www.garethstevens.com. For a free color catalog of all our high-quality books, call toll free 1-800-542-2595 or fax 1-877-542-2596.

Library of Congress Cataloging-in-Publication Data

Palmer, Kristin.
Wild weather trivia / by Kristin Palmer.
  p. cm. — (Ultimate trivia challenge)
Includes index.
ISBN 978-1-4339-8305-4 (pbk.)
ISBN 978-1-4339-8306-1 (6-pack)
ISBN 978-1-4339-8304-7 (library binding)
1. Weather—Miscellanea—Juvenile literature. 2. Weather—Juvenile literature. I. Title.
QC981.3 P35 2014
551.5—dc23

First Edition

Published in 2014 by
Gareth Stevens Publishing
111 East 14th Street, Suite 349
New York, NY 10003

Copyright © 2014 Gareth Stevens Publishing

Designer: Andrea Davison-Bartolotta
Editor: Greg Roza

Photo credits: Cover, p. 1 (hail) Habrda/Shutterstock.com, (lightning) Steshkin Yevgeniy/ Shutterstock.com, (hurricane) Guido Amrein/Shutterstock.com; p. 4 Ron Chapple Studios/Thinkstock; pp. 5 (top left, top right, bottom right), 16, 18, 23 iStockphoto/Thinkstock; p. 5 (bottom left) Comstock/ Thinkstock; p. 6 Kaveh Kazemi/Getty Images; pp. 7 (main), 15 (map), 21 (satellite image) courtesy of NOAA via Wikimedia Commons; pp. 7 (inset), 26, 27, 28 courtesy of NASA via Wikimedia Commons; p. 8 Sam Panthaky/AFP/Getty Images; p. 9 zeber/Shutterstock.com; p. 10 Oliver J. Davis Photography/ Flickr/Getty Images; p. 11 Photos.com/Thinkstock; p. 12 Bronwyn Photo/Shutterstock.com; p. 13 Alan Majchrowicz/The Image Bank/Getty Images; p. 14 courtesy of Christine Schultz/National Science Foundation; p. 15 (arrow) vector-RGB/Shutterstock.com; p. 17 Ethan Miller/Getty Images; p. 19 (both) courtesy of NOAA; pp. 20, 21 (map) courtesy of Wikimedia Commons; p. 22 Robert Armstrong/ Photolibrary/Getty Images; p. 24 Minerva Studio/Shutterstock.com; p. 25 Dustie/Shutterstock.com; p. 29 Digital Vision/Thinkstock.

Printed in the United States of America

CPSIA compliance information: Batch #CS13GS: For further information contact Gareth Stevens, New York, New York at 1-800-542-2595.

CONTENTS

Extreme Earth. 4

Hot and Cold 6

Rainfall. 8

Fog. 11

Snowfall 12

Wind 14

Stormy Weather 16

Tropical Cyclones. 20

Tornadoes 23

Space Weather!. 26

Weather Watchers 29

Glossary. 30

For More Information 31

Index 32

Words in the glossary appear in **bold** type the first time they are used in the text.

EXTREME EARTH

Earth is a planet of **extremes**. It has frozen **tundra** and red-hot deserts. It has sunny beaches and soggy rainforests. It has tall mountains and deep canyons. Earth is also home to many weather extremes. On any given day, it's raining somewhere and snowing somewhere else.

Earth is the only planet we know of so far that supports life. Despite the many different kinds of extreme weather, people have managed to survive and flourish. Do you want to learn more about Earth's extreme weather? Then read on!

Earth

These are just a few of the weather extremes found on Earth.

HOT AND COLD

What is the hottest place on Earth?

From 2003 to 2009, scientists at the University of Montana used **satellites** to measure surface temperatures around the world. For 5 of those 7 years, the highest temperatures in the world were in the Lut Desert of Iran. In 2005, the land temperature there reached 159°F (71°C).

The Lut Desert is considered an abiotic zone. That is a place where few or no living things can survive.

Antarctica

Vostok Station

What is the coldest place on Earth?

Vostok, Antarctica, has been home to a Russian scientific research station since 1957. Scientists from all over the world have worked there. In 1983, the coldest temperature ever measured on Earth was recorded at Vostok Station. The temperature dropped to –128.6°F (–89.2°C).

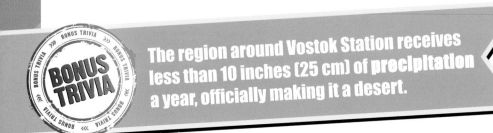

BONUS TRIVIA

The region around Vostok Station receives less than 10 inches (25 cm) of precipitation a year, officially making it a desert.

RAINFALL

What area holds the record for most rainfall in 1 year?

Areas around the Indian Ocean experience the rainiest seasons of any regions on Earth. The summer **monsoon** causes extreme rainfall and flooding in India. Between the beginning of August 1860 and the end of July 1861, Cherrapunji, India, received 86.84 feet (26.47 m) of rainfall.

A bus travels on a flooded street in Ahmedabad, India, in August 2007.

What is the record for most rainfall in 1 day?

Madagascar
Réunion

In January 1966, a tropical cyclone—or hurricane—battered islands across the southern Indian Ocean. On January 7 and 8, 71.8 inches (182.4 cm) of rain fell on the French island of Réunion, which lies east of Madagascar.

BONUS TRIVIA

The island of Réunion also holds several other rainfall records, all of which were the result of tropical cyclones.

record	location	year	rainfall
most rain in 24 hours	Foc-Foc, Réunion	1966	71.8 inches (182.4 cm)
most rain in 48 hours	Aurère, Réunion	1958	97.1 inches (246.7 cm)
most rain in 72 hours	Commerson, Réunion	2007	154.7 inches (392.9 cm)
most rain in 10 days	Commerson, Réunion	1980	223.5 inches (567.7 cm)

What is the driest place on Earth?

The Atacama Desert of Chile receives very little rainfall. Just north of the desert, the city of Arica receives an average 0.03 inch (0.08 cm) of rainfall a year, which is the lowest in the world. No rainfall was recorded for Arica from October 1903 to January 1918—a period of over 14 years.

There are areas of the Atacama Desert where no one has ever reported seeing rainfall.

BONUS TRIVIA

Scientists believe that some regions of the Atacama Desert have been "hyperarid" (superdry) for nearly 40 million years.

FOG

Where is the foggiest place on Earth?

Grand Banks is an area of the Atlantic Ocean near the coast of Newfoundland, Canada, where a warm current meets a cold current. This makes Grand Banks the foggiest place in the world. The nearby coastal town of Argentia, Newfoundland, has over 200 days of fog a year.

SNOWFALL

What is the record for most snowfall in 24 hours?

At 2:30 p.m. on April 14, 1921, heavy snow began falling on Silver Lake, Colorado. By that time the next day, Silver Lake was buried under 75.8 inches (192.5 cm) of snow! The snow continued nonstop for a total of 32.5 hours, resulting in 95 inches (241.3 cm) of fresh snow on Silver Lake.

Ninety-five inches is nearly 8 feet (2.4 m). That's taller than anyone you've ever met!

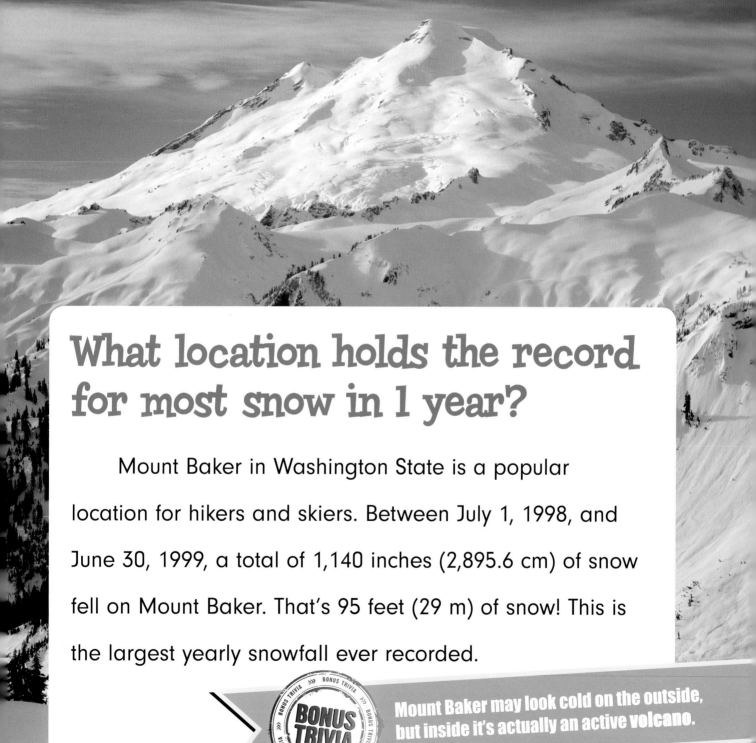

What location holds the record for most snow in 1 year?

Mount Baker in Washington State is a popular location for hikers and skiers. Between July 1, 1998, and June 30, 1999, a total of 1,140 inches (2,895.6 cm) of snow fell on Mount Baker. That's 95 feet (29 m) of snow! This is the largest yearly snowfall ever recorded.

BONUS TRIVIA

Mount Baker may look cold on the outside, but inside it's actually an active volcano.

WIND

What is the windiest place on Earth?

Port Martin, Antarctica, has an average yearly wind speed of 40 miles (64 km) per hour. Port Martin experiences gale force 8 wind speed on more than 100 days every year. That means the wind is blowing between 39 and 46 miles (63 and 74 km) per hour.

BONUS TRIVIA

Port Martin winds are called katabatic winds. They're caused when a cold slope cools the air above it. The air sinks and speeds up as it flows downhill.

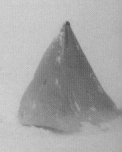

When the jet stream over the United States dips south, it brings the cold northern climate with it.

How fast are jet-stream winds?

Jet streams are bands of strong winds in the upper **atmosphere**. They flow west to east, forming a border between warm air and cold air. Jet streams close to the poles are stronger than those farther away. A "polar jet" can reach speeds greater than 275 miles (440 km) per hour.

STORMY WEATHER

How hot is a bolt of lightning?

A bolt of lightning is a sudden **discharge** of electrical energy in the sky. It can go from a cloud to the ground, from the ground to a cloud, or it can occur within a cloud. A lightning bolt heats the air around it by as much as 50,000°F (27,760°C).

BONUS TRIVIA

A bolt of lightning is about five times hotter than the surface of the sun.

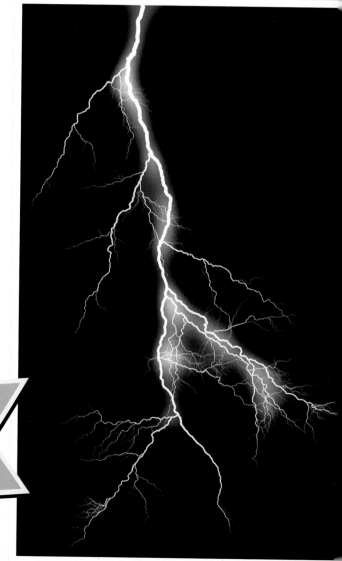

How often does lightning strike Earth?

Weather services around the world, such as the US National Oceanic and Atmospheric Administration (NOAA), monitor storms and lightning strikes. Lightning hits the United States 25 million times a year. Scientists **estimate** that Earth as a whole is struck by more than 100 lightning bolts every second.

What is the number one cause of thunderstorm-related deaths?

Flash floods cause a lot of damage in a short amount of time.

Thunderstorms can be very dangerous. Lightning kills an average of 54 people every year in the United States. However, **flash floods** caused by thunderstorms kill an average of 127 people every year in the United States. Just 6 inches (15 cm) of rushing water can knock a person down.

What is the biggest hailstone on record?

A hailstone is a ball of ice formed during some kinds of thunderstorms. Winds hold the ice up in the clouds where it gets bigger until it becomes so heavy it crashes to the ground. The largest hailstone on record was 8 inches (20.3 cm) across and weighed 1.9 pounds (0.9 kg).

BONUS TRIVIA

The record-setting hailstone—which fell in Vivian, South Dakota, on July 23, 2010—melted a little before it was measured. So, it was originally larger than 8 inches across.

TROPICAL CYCLONES

Which hurricane lasted the longest?

the path of Hurricane John

For 31 days in 1994, Hurricane John traveled from the eastern Pacific Ocean into the western Pacific Ocean and then back to the eastern Pacific. Not only is it the longest-lasting hurricane on record, it also traveled the farthest distance of any recorded hurricane: 8,252 miles (13,280 km).

BONUS TRIVIA

Depending where they're located, tropical cyclones can be called different things. When the 1994 tropical cyclone was in the eastern Pacific, it was called Hurricane John. In the western Pacific, it was called Typhoon John.

What is the greatest wind speed ever recorded for a tropical cyclone?

On April 10, 1996, Tropical Cyclone Olivia slammed into Barrow Island, Australia, bringing with it winds that reached a speed of 253 miles (407 km) per hour. Olivia's winds slowed as it raced across the continent through the next 2 days.

the path of Tropical Cyclone Olivia

Which tropical cyclone was the deadliest in recorded history?

In 1970, a powerful tropical cyclone hit the coasts of

East Pakistan (now Bangladesh) and India. The storm destroyed farmland and villages throughout the area. Although reports differ, deaths resulting from the storm are thought to be at least 300,000 and perhaps as much as 500,000.

BONUS TRIVIA

After the 1970 cyclone, slow relief response from the Pakistani government helped lead to a civil war. Soon after, East Pakistan seceded, or broke away, from Pakistan and became Bangladesh.

TORNADOES

What city has been hit by the most recorded tornadoes?

Oklahoma City, Oklahoma, is right in the middle of Tornado Alley, which is an area of the Great Plains where tornadoes commonly form. More than 100 tornadoes have hit Oklahoma City since record keeping began in 1893. Three tornadoes hit the city in April of that year.

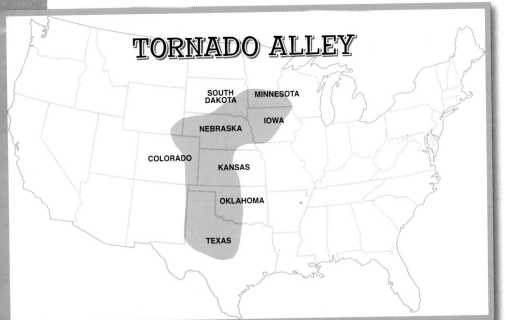

TORNADO ALLEY

SOUTH DAKOTA
MINNESOTA
IOWA
NEBRASKA
COLORADO
KANSAS
OKLAHOMA
TEXAS

What is the fastest wind speed ever recorded on Earth?

Tornadoes create the greatest wind speeds of any weather **phenomenon** on Earth. On May 3, 1999, a tornado destroyed about 250 houses in a suburb of Oklahoma City, Oklahoma. Scientists studying the tornado recorded a wind speed of 318 miles (512 km) per hour.

Tornadoes have a funnel shape. They are wide on top and narrow on the bottom.

What is the record for most tornadoes in 24 hours?

Between April 25 and April 28, 2011, approximately 362 tornadoes were reported during a storm that stretched from Texas to New York. During this time, 312 tornadoes were spotted during one 24-hour period. This broke the previous record of 148 tornadoes between April 3 and 4, 1974.

BONUS TRIVIA

April 2011 set a record for most tornado reports for a single month with 753.

SPACE WEATHER!

Where in our solar system is the weather most similar to Earth's weather?

Saturn's moon Titan is very different from Earth. However, the weather on Titan is oddly similar to Earth's weather. The solar system's second-largest moon has four seasons. It also features lakes, clouds, and rain. The liquid on Titan isn't water, though. It's a liquid called methane.

Many scientists think Titan could possibly support some simple forms of life.

BONUS TRIVIA

On Earth, methane is a flammable gas. On Titan, however, the temperature is much colder, which allows methane to exist in liquid form.

The dark spot on Neptune is a storm almost as big as Earth.

Where are the fastest winds in the solar system found?

Neptune is the farthest planet from the sun in our solar system. It looks bright blue because of the methane in its atmosphere. Neptune features storms and white clouds. It also has the fastest winds in the solar system. Wind speed on Neptune can reach about 1,500 miles (2,400 km) per hour.

Where is the biggest storm in the solar system?

Jupiter's Great Red Spot is the largest storm in the solar system. It's about 12,500 miles (20,000 km) long and spins in much the same way a hurricane spins. The Great Red Spot has been on Jupiter at least 400 years, when it was first viewed by scientists.

Winds in the Great Red Spot regularly reach 300 miles (480 km) per hour.

Weather Watchers

You now know a lot of cool weather trivia you can use to amaze your friends—from Earth's driest location to the windiest place in the solar system. But why stop there? What is the longest **blizzard** on record? Which location boasts the largest temperature change in just 24 hours? Keep searching for the answers!

GLOSSARY

atmosphere: the mixture of gases that surround a planet

blizzard: a heavy snowstorm with strong winds

discharge: to lose an electrical charge

estimate: to make a careful guess about an answer based on the known facts

extreme: great or severe

flash flood: a sudden flood usually caused by heavy rain

monsoon: a seasonal change in wind direction resulting in a change in precipitation

phenomenon: a fact or an event that is observed

precipitation: rain, snow, sleet, or hail

satellite: an object that circles Earth in order to collect and send information or aid in communication

tundra: cold northern lands that lack forests and have permanently frozen soil below the surface

volcano: an opening in a planet's surface through which hot, liquid rock sometimes flows

For More Information

Books

Hynes, Margaret. *Extreme Weather*. New York, NY: Kingfisher, 2011.

Snedeker, Joseph. *The Everything Kids' Weather Book*. Avon, MA: Adams Media, 2012.

Websites

The Weather Channel Kids!
theweatherchannelkids.com
Learn more about weather and play weather-related games.

Weather Wiz Kids
www.weatherwizkids.com
This website, designed by a meteorologist, takes an in-depth look at many weather phenomena and related topics.

INDEX

Atacama Desert, Chile 10

Cherrapunji, India 8

coldest temperatures 7

desert 4, 7

flash floods 18

flooding 8, 18

fog 11

Grand Banks 11

Great Red Spot 28

hailstone 19

highest temperatures 6

hurricane 9, 20, 28

Hurricane John 20

jet streams 15

Jupiter 28

katabatic winds 14

lightning 16, 17, 18

Lut Desert, Iran 6

Mount Baker, Washington 13

Neptune 27

Newfoundland 11

Oklahoma City, Oklahoma 23, 24

Port Martin, Antarctica 14

rain 4, 8, 9, 10, 26

Réunion 9

Silver Lake, Colorado 12

snow 4, 12, 13

thunderstorms 18, 19

Titan 26

Tornado Alley 23

tornadoes 23, 24, 25

tropical cyclone 9, 20, 21, 22

Tropical Cyclone Olivia 21

Typhoon John 20

Vostok Station, Antarctica 7

winds 14, 15, 19, 21, 24, 27, 28, 29